FAMOUS U.S. SPY PLANES

GEORGE SULLIVAN

U.S. AIR FORCE

DODD, MEAD & COMPANY
New York

Other titles in this series

Famous Air Force Fighters
Famous Air Force Bombers
Famous Navy Fighter Planes
Famous Navy Attack Planes

Library of Congress Cataloging-in-Publication Data

Sullivan, George, date
    Famous U.S. spy planes.

    Summary: Examines the characteristics and functions of various types of spy planes developed in the United States from World War I to the present day.
    1. Reconnaissance aircraft—United States—Juvenile literature. [1. Reconnaissance aircraft. 2. Airplanes, Military] I. Title. II. Title: Famous US spy planes.
UG1242.R4S85   1987   358.4′5′0973   86-32857
ISBN 0-396-08844-9

INTRODUCTION

Every night and day, from bases scattered across the face of the globe, swift, sleek aircraft take to the air on information-gathering missions. They are spy planes. Their operations are blanketed in the deepest secrecy.

Spying from the air has been going on for a very long time, ever since 1794, when a hot-air balloon was used to observe a battlefield in France. As for the airplane, it has been used for spying almost from the day the Wright Brothers got the first one to fly. That was in 1903. A dependable aerial camera was invented three years later. The history of the plane and camera have been mixed together ever since.

One thing about aerial spying, none of the spying nations ever use the word "spy" or the term "spy plane" in describing what these aircraft do. They say they're involved in scouting, observation, or patrol. They claim they're being used for surveillance, a French word that means "watching over." Or they say their planes are being used for reconnaissance, another French word, which means "searching for useful information."

But it all adds up to the same thing—spying.

There are many different types of spy planes. These include specially designed aircraft that are equipped with sophisticated cameras and different kinds of sensing devices. These planes collect information.

There are AEW (Airborne Early Warning) aircraft. Developed by the U.S. Navy in the 1940s, these warn of hostile planes and ships.

There are also big AWACS (Airborne Warning and Control Systems) aircraft. Not only do these sound the alarm when they detect incoming enemy planes, they have electronic equipment that enables them to direct any land or sea battle that then might occur.

The pages that follow examine the best-known spy planes developed in the United States. The parade begins with aircraft of World War I, continues through World War II and the introduction of jets, and ends with modern-day planes, aircraft that are able to fly faster and climb higher than any other planes in the world.

The author is grateful to many people who helped him in the preparation of this book. Special thanks are due Larry Wilson, Smithsonian Institution; Lt. June Green, Department of the Air Force; Jeanne J. Thomas, Department of the Navy; Barbara Weiner, USS *Intrepid* Sea-Air-Space Museum; Marilyn Phipps, The Boeing Co.; Eric Schulzinger, Lockheed-California Co.; Bob Harwood, Lois Lovisolo, Grumman Corporation; Jack Isabel, General Dynamics; Francene Crum, Martin Marietta Corp.; and Francesca Kurti, TLC Custom Labs.

CONTENTS

Curtiss Jenny had a cruising speed of 75 miles an hour, more with a tail wind.

CURTISS JN

The first time the United States used an airplane to gather information about what might be called "enemy forces" occurred in 1916. The airplane was a Curtiss JN, or Jenny, as it was nicknamed.

On March 9, 1916, Mexican revolutionist Pancho Villa, leading several hundred armed and mounted men, crossed the border and raided the little town of Columbus, New Mexico. Seventeen American soldiers and civilians were killed. Many more Americans were injured.

The federal government ordered General John Pershing to lead an expedition into Mexico to find Villa and bring him back. Pershing asked for the assistance of the Aviation Section of the Army's Signal Corps, which had been supplied with Jennies.

The planes were hardly fit for military service. Their only weapons consisted of pistols or rifles that some of the pilots happened to carry. For bombs, they were armed with three-inch shells which had been intended for use by the artillery.

Some of the planes were forced down by engine trouble and never got to Mexico. Others got lost. But the planes that did arrive successfully carried out reconnaissance and photographic missions.

Aerial photography in 1916 was primitive by comparison with the methods used today. The photographer, belted in by a leather strap, stood in the Jenny's rear cockpit. He held a camera that weighed between eight and ten pounds. He looked through a viewer with cross hairs and fired away. But he didn't fire for long. The camera's magazine held film enough for only twelve photos. When the photographer had snapped that many, he had to stop and reload.

Jennies flew many thousands of miles in support of General Pershing's expedition into Mexico. It is doubtful, however, whether the photos that were taken helped very much. Pershing's force advanced some 400 miles into Mexico, but was unable to capture Villa. Pershing and his troops were ordered home early in February of 1917.

From that not very glorious beginning, the Jenny went on to become one of the most noted planes in the history of American aviation. More than 5,500 Jennies were built. It was the plane the U.S. Army used to train its aviators, and photos taken from Jenny cockpits were used in mapping vast areas of the United States.

Other Data (Model JN-3)
Wingspan: 43 ft., 7⅜ in.
Length: 27 ft., 4 in.
Power Plant: One 90-hp water-cooled Curtiss OX-5
Takeoff Weight: 2,130 lb.
Maximum Speed: 75 mph at sea level

Jenny was a workhorse plane in aviation's early days; here one takes on a load of mail.

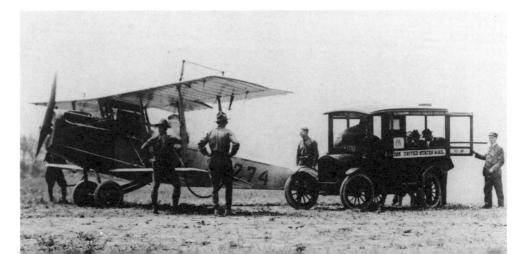

DE HAVILLAND DH-4

Nicknamed "The Liberty Plane," the DH-4 was produced in greater quantity by American manufacturers during World War I than any other aircraft. A total of 4,846 DH-4s were built.

But only a relatively few planes were shipped to France, where the war was mainly fought. At the time the armistice was declared in 1918, the United States had several thousand DH-4s on hand. "For a number of years after the war," wrote Lt. George W. Goddard in his book, *Overview*, "one could crack up a DH-4 and, if he walked away from the wreck, call the supply depot and simply order a new one."

Many of the DH-4s were put to use in peacetime taking aerial photographs. County, state, and federal agencies needed photographs of highways,

DH-4 was said to be poorly designed, too heavy and quick to overheat. But it played an important role in post-World War I aviation.

Army aviators of the 1920s, dressed to ward off extreme cold encountered at high altitudes, pose with their DH-4.

rivers, harbors, and other such features. The photos were used in producing new maps or correcting old ones.

During the mapping missions, the DH-4s operated at an altitude of from 16,000 to 18,000 feet. It took the plane, heavily loaded with photographic gear, a full hour to get to that altitude. The upward climb, plus the continuing use of maximum power to stay at that level, put an enormous strain on the engine.

This was a time before airplanes were fitted with oxygen masks, so pilots had to guard against oxygen starvation, which could cause a loss of consciousness. They also had to cope with the constant roar of the engine, which was less than six feet from the open cockpit.

In 1923, Lt. George Goddard, a pioneer in aerial photography, was given an assignment that had a wartime flavor to it. It had to do with a treaty between the United States and Mexico concerning the use of water from the Colorado River. The Mexicans were suspected of using the water to irrigate more land than they were entitled to irrigate, and were thus thought to be violating the treaty. Goddard was assigned to photograph secretly the area in question from his DH-4.

It was a dangerous mission. Not long before, two pilots flying border patrol had gotten lost and landed in Mexico. They were beaten and thrown

Not every DH-4 landing was as smooth as this one; indeed, crack-ups were not uncommon.

in jail. It took the U.S. State Department nearly a month to win their release.

Goddard, who was to take the photos, and his pilot took off from an airfield near Yuma, Arizona, and headed south. The three-hour mission went off without a hitch.

The next day, the two men were not so lucky. They had been photographing over Mexico for about two hours when the plane's engine began to sputter. The pilot turned and headed for the border, ten or fifteen miles away. Suddenly the engine gave a final burst and quit dead.

10

Down the plane glided. The two men did not speak. The only sound was the wind whistling through the braces between the wings.

The pilot landed the plane in a potato field. Though it tilted up onto its nose, neither man was hurt. They had managed to cross the border with less than a thousand feet to spare.

Goddard never learned what happened to the photographs he took. Nevertheless, the mission was important. It marked the first time that a United States reconnaissance plane had overflown a foreign country with whom the nation was at peace. It was not to be the last time.

Besides their use in map making (and an occasional secret mission), DH-4s were also used to pioneer many of the aviation routes in the United States. The plane continued in service into the early 1930s.

Other Data (Model DH-4)
Wingspan: 42 ft., 6 in.
Length: 29 ft., 11 in.
Power Plant: One 420-hp Liberty
Loaded Weight: 4,297 lb.
Maximum Speed: 124 mph

Lt. George W. Goddard made important contributions in the development of aerial photography. This photo dates to 1922.

DOUGLAS O-2

Produced in the mid-1920s to replace the DH-4, the Douglas O-2 was another of the Army's first spy planes. Its chief mission was to observe and photograph enemy forces and installations. Since the United States was at peace at the time the Douglas plane was developed, it was given other assignments. These included aerial mapping, gathering weather information and, later, carrying the mail.

Powered by a 400-hp Liberty engine, the O-2 proved much superior to the DH-4 in the way it performed. The aircraft carried a crew of two, the pilot in the front seat, the photographer behind him.

The O-2 had a safety feature unusual for the day. The two wing fuel tanks, each of which was

O-2 was superior to earlier planes in strength, construction, and performance.

Besides seeing duty as an observation plane, the O-2 also served as a pioneer mailplane.

made of aluminum and held sixty gallons, could be dropped by the pilot should a crash-landing loom. A smaller ten-gallon tank in the upper wing assured that the plane would not be completely fuel-less.

The O-2 also boasted the latest in flying instruments, including an advanced altimeter for measuring altitude. But the device was not always reliable. Take the case of Lt. Frank Klein. One summer morning in 1936, Klein took off in his O-2 to gather weather information. Ten minutes after takeoff, Klein ran into a severe thunderstorm. It was so violent that Klein decided to turn the plane around and head back to the airfield.

Since his view of the ground was now blotted out by thick clouds, Klein had to navigate by his instruments. His altimeter read 2,000 feet. Suddenly the plane brushed against something solid. Thinking it could only be another aircraft, Klein checked his parachute, unbuckled his seat belt, and got set to make his escape.

When he peered into the darkness below, he could not believe his eyes. A man, his robe flapping in the wind and rain, and holding a lantern in one hand, was staring up at him. Klein thought perhaps heaven's gate had opened and St. Peter was about to greet him.

"Are you all right?" the man shouted. Then Klein looked about and realized that the plane had glided into a farmer's orchard. The impact he felt was a tree he had bumped. Before he made his exit, Klein looked down at his instruments. The altimeter was still reporting "2,000 feet."

Other Data (Model O2-H)
Wingspan: 39 ft., 8 in.
Length: 28 ft., 11 in.
Power Plant: One 400-hp Liberty
Loaded Weight: 4,960 lb.
Maximum Speed: 130 mph (estimated)

Fairchild's C-8 represented a big step forward in the development of reconnaissance aircraft.

FAIRCHILD C-8

Sherman Fairchild went into the business of making airplanes in the mid-1920s. Before the decade ended, he had introduced the C-8, the first aircraft designed especially for photoreconnaissance, the photographing of enemy forces and troops during wartime.

The plane was a big improvement over the DH-4 and Douglas O-2. A high-wing monoplane, the C-8 offered a cockpit with all-around visibility. The spacious cabin could hold three photographers plus the pilot. The aircraft had a range of 500 miles.

On each side of the plane's fuselage were glass doors through which cameras could be aimed. And there were openings in the cabin floor, also for camera placement.

Fairchild not only designed and manufactured airplanes; he was in the forefront of the development of aerial cameras.

During the early 1920s, Fairchild's K-3 camera became standard equipment on all U.S. reconnaissance planes. It was electrically driven, not hand wound. It provided sharper pictures without any distortion. Although it occasionally jammed because of the plane's vibration, it was hailed as the most advanced camera of the day.

Despite the excellent equipment available to photographers, map making was no easy task. Once the pilot had reached the proper altitude, he had to fly straight and level in one direction, make a 180-degree turn, and then fly straight and level in the direction opposite. All the while, the photographer would be snapping pictures. The strips of film that resulted were planned so that their images overlapped. When the strips were pieced together, they formed a photographic mosaic, a complete representation of the area covered.

The pioneer aviators who flew the early De Havilland DH-4s, Douglas O-2Hs, and Fairchild C-8s on map-making expeditions are unsung heroes. Many gave up their lives in airplane accidents. Their work helped to define the North American continent in a scope and detail not previously known.

Other Data (Model C-8)
Wingspan: 50 ft.
Length: 33 ft.
Power Plant: One 450-hp Pratt & Whitney R-985 Wasp Junior
Loaded Weight: 4,968 lb.
Maximum Speed: 142 mph

A C-8, bearing the symbol of the U.S. Army Air Force, at an airfield typical of the time.

A battleship's catapult fires an SOC Seagull into the air.

CURTISS SOC SEAGULL

First flown in 1934, the Curtiss SOC Seagull served Navy battleships and cruisers as a scouting and observation plane. Its job was to fly ahead of the fleet, searching for ships and aircraft that could be classed as unfriendly. Information the pilot obtained would be radioed back to the fleet.

The Seagull was so successful as a scout and observation plane that it was pressed into service during World War II, and it managed to outlast even the aircraft that was designed to replace it.

When serving aboard a battleship or cruiser, the Seagull was launched from the ship by means of a catapult. The plane would first be loaded onto a launching cradle and then the catapult would be fired, hurling the aircraft into the air. Sometimes gunpowder was used as the propellant; other times, compressed air.

Once it had accomplished its mission, the plane would alight in the water next to the ship it served. A crane would then hoist it aboard. The Seagull had a range of 675 miles.

The aircraft could also be equipped with wheeled landing gear for service aboard aircraft carriers. But it was as a float plane that the aircraft won the highest praise.

Production of the Seagull was scheduled to end in 1938. A monoplane version of the plane had been designed to replace it. However, the new version of the plane was not nearly as successful as the old, and had to be taken out of service in 1944. By that time, World War II was raging. The old Seagull airplanes were made shipshape and put back into service. Not until after the war ended were they finally permitted to retire.

Other Data (Model SOC-1)
Wingspan: 36 ft.
Length: 31 ft., 5 in.
Power Plant: One 600-hp Pratt & Whitney R-1340 Wasp
Loaded Weight: 5,430 lb.
Maximum Speed: 165 mph at 5,000 ft.

The Seagull could be fitted out with wheeled landing gear for use aboard aircraft carriers.

CURTISS F9C SPARROWHAWK

The F9C Sparrowhawk holds a special place in aviation history. It was the only aircraft to serve aboard the huge rigid airships, the *Akron* and *Macon*, that the Navy began operating in 1931.

The airships themselves, which had been produced for the Navy by the Goodyear Zeppelin Company of Akron, Ohio, were intended to be airborne scouting platforms, keeping watch over the approaches to the United States. The Sparrowhawks increased the range of the airships even farther. The planes traveled far and wide from their mother ships, reporting any sightings to the dirigibles by radio.

Four Sparrowhawks were assigned to each airship, although there was room aboard for only one at a time. Each airplane was fitted with a special "skyhook" attached to its upper fuselage. Flying at exactly the speed of the airship, the pilot would guide the hook onto the horizontal bar of a recovery trapeze that hung down from beneath the airship.

Once the hookup had been completed, the pilot would cut the plane's engine. Then the plane would be raised into the open belly of the airship where it was stored on a special rack.

To launch a Sparrowhawk, the procedure was reversed. The plane was lowered from the airship with its engine running, then released to become airborne.

A tiny Sparrowhawk "hooks up" with the airship it serves.

The system worked very efficiently. But the Navy's airship program was stung by tragedy. The *Akron* was lost in a storm at sea in 1933. A similar accident claimed the *Macon* two years later.

Without any airship from which to operate, the

Sparrowhawks were assigned to Navy air bases. In 1939, the one remaining Sparrowhawk was transferred by the Navy to the Smithsonian Institution. Today that plane is on exhibition at the National Air and Space Museum in Washington, D.C.

Other Data (Model F9C-2)
Wingspan: 25 ft., 5 in.
Length: 20 ft., 7 in.
Power Plant: One 438-hp Wright Whirlwind
Loaded Weight: 2,770 lb.
Maximum Speed: 176 mph

Sparrowhawks fly in formation above an airship hangar at Moffett Field, Sunnyvale, California.

VOUGHT OS2U KINGFISHER

When the United States was thrust into World War II in 1941, the Navy had several scouting and observation planes available. Vought's OS2U Kingfisher quickly proved to be the best. Sturdy and dependable, the trim all-metal monoplane represented a big step forward over the spindly biplanes of earlier days.

The OS2U flew for the first time on July 20, 1938. The plane entered service in August, 1940. It could be fitted with either wheels or landing-float gear. In the latter case, the plane was catapulted from battleships or cruisers. The first Kingfishers were assigned to the Pensacola Naval Air Station, the Pearl Harbor Battle Force, and the battleships *Colorado* and *Mississippi*.

The Kingfisher was not a fast plane; its maximum speed was only 164 miles an hour. It had a cruising range of 805 miles.

Assigned to the Pacific Theater of Operations, the Kingfisher was given many duties. It searched for Japanese submarines, shadowed enemy surface forces, and gathered information about land-based

The Kingfisher was not only valuable as a scout and observation plane, but it helped in rescuing countless airmen downed by the enemy.

installations and operations. It was the first plane to earn billing as "the eyes of the fleet."

The Kingfisher also won high praise as a rescue aircraft. Indeed, many Kingfisher crews were decorated for bravery for snatching downed airmen from waters under Japanese control while being raked with heavy fire.

The Kingfisher's most notable feat was in rescuing Capt. Eddie Rickenbacker, America's best-known World War I ace. (An ace is a pilot who has downed at least five enemy aircraft). On a special flight for the government in 1942, Rickenbacker had to ditch his plane in the Pacific. He and two crew members spent three weeks on a small raft before they were spotted by a Kingfisher. The survivors proved to be too big a load for the plane and it could not take off. So the pilot simply taxied forty miles to the nearest land.

A total of 1,006 Kingfishers were built. The final plane came off the assembly line in 1942. But Kingfishers remained on active duty until VJ Day, August 14, 1945, the day that Japan accepted Allied surrender terms.

Other Data (Model OS2U-3)
Wingspan: 35 ft., 11 in.
Length: 33 ft., 10 in.
Power Plant: One 450-hp Pratt & Whitney R-985 Wasp Junior
Loaded Weight: 6,000 lb.
Maximum Speed: 164 mph at 5,500 ft.

A total of 1,006 Kingfishers were produced for the Navy during World War II.

CURTISS SC SEAHAWK

In June, 1942, only seven months after the Japanese had bombed Pearl Harbor and plunged the United States into World War II, the Navy issued a call for an improved scout plane. The Curtiss SC Seahawk was the result.

A stubby, low-wing monoplane, the single-seat Seahawk was one of the most efficient of the Navy's wartime scouts. It had a range of 600 miles, could climb at the rate of 2,500 feet per minute, cruise at 125 miles an hour, and when necessary, speed along at 313 miles per hour, which was excellent for its day.

Like other aircraft of its type, the Seahawk spied upon enemy ships and shore-based operations. But the Seahawk was a scout plane with a sting. The aircraft was equipped with two forward-firing .50-caliber machine guns and under-the-wing bomb racks, each capable of toting a 300-pound bomb.

While the Seahawk was produced with wheeled landing gear only, it could be converted for use as a float plane by installing a large central float and

About 500 Curtiss Seahawks saw duty as Navy scout planes during World War II.

Although it came off the Curtiss assembly line with a wheeled landing gear, the Seahawk could be converted for use as a float plane.

smaller wing-tip floats. The conversion kit enabled the Seahawk to operate not only from land bases but from aircraft carriers, and from battleships as well.

But the Seahawk was the last of the Navy's scout planes to have this versatility. By the end of World War II, float planes were headed the way of biplanes and open cockpits.

The first Seahawks were delivered to the carrier *Guam* in October, 1944. A total of 576 were built. The Seahawk had no role in postwar aviation.

Those that happened to be in service when World War II ended on August 14, 1945, were soon scrapped.

Other Data (Model SC-1)
Wingspan: 41 ft.
Length: 36 ft., 4½ in.
Power Plant: One 1,350-hp Wright Cyclone
Loaded Weight: 9,000 lb.
Maximum Speed: 313 mph at 28,600 ft.

23

Known for its spectacular diving speed, Lockheed's Lightning was the most widely used reconnaissance plane of World War II.

LOCKHEED F-4, F-5 LIGHTNING

During World War II, the Army Air Force converted several different fighters for use as photoreconnaissance planes. The most successful conversion involved the Lockheed P-38 Lightning, "the fork-tailed devil," as German pilots called it. More than 1,400 P-38s became F-4 and F-5 camera planes. (The F-4 was fitted out with four cameras, the F-5 with five.) They served everywhere the war was fought.

The P-38 had a nose compartment that held four .50-caliber machine guns. In converting the plane to photoreconnaissance use, these were removed and forward-looking cameras were installed in their place. But the alteration weakened the plane's nose. The vibrations that resulted once the plane was airborne made the photos blurry.

The solution was to make the camera plane's nose bigger and stronger. It was so much bigger that it could hold another crew member and it earned the plane the nickname "droop snoot."

With its old nose or the new one, the Lightning had spectacular diving speed. One pilot took the plane to 43,000 feet and dove straight down to 25,000 feet before leveling off. His air speed indicator hit 780 miles per hour.

This quality made the Lightning an exceptional reconnaissance plane. The pilot could dive down out of the clouds right on target, take the photos,

The nose of the Lightning held several cameras, each operated by the pilot by means of a switch box.

and suddenly be gone. Vast areas could be photographed in the blink of an eye.

After World War II ended in 1945, Lightnings quickly disappeared from the scene. But their contribution as the Army's most widely used reconnaissance plane will not be forgotten.

Other Data (Model P-38L)
Wingspan: 52 ft.
Length: 37 ft., 10 in.
Power Plant: Two 1,425-hp liquid-cooled Allisons
Loaded Weight: 17,500 lb.
Maximum Speed: 414 mph at 25,000 ft.

LOCKHEED FP-80 SHOOTING STAR

Although not a fast-looking plane, Lockheed's P-80 Shooting Star was the first operational jet fighter to enter service with the U.S. Air Force. The FP-80, the camera-carrying version of the plane, thrust the science of photoreconnaissance into the jet age.

The P-80 was designed, built, and tested during World War II. Four P-80s were delivered to Europe early in 1945 and were demonstrated for flight crews in England and Italy. The war in Europe ended with the surrender of Germany on May 7, 1945, and the planes never saw action in combat.

In the years following the war, the P-80 was fitted with a new nose and camera gear to become the FP-80. A port was provided in the nose through

The FP-80 Shooting Star, the first jet-powered photoreconnaissance aircraft.

which the cameras were aimed. Adjustable racks were provided for cameras of different types.

Aerial photography of the day was based upon the strip camera. It automatically adjusted the speed of the film moving across the camera's focal plane to the speed of the airplane in flight. Clear and sharp photos, without the slightest blurring, were the result.

But would the strip camera be workable in the FP-80, a plane traveling at speeds greater than 500 miles an hour? A test was ordered to find out. One FP-80 was ordered to fly directly east at 500 miles an hour. A second FP-80 flew directly west at the same speed and at an altitude that put it slightly higher than the first plane. The second plane carried a camera. At the instant the two planes passed each other in the sky, the camera plane took a photograph.

The camera passed the test with flying colors. When the film was developed, it showed such rich detail that individual rivets in the wings of the lower plane were visible.

Close to 400 Shooting Stars were assigned to operational units in Korea when the Korean War broke out in 1950. Some of these planes were FP-80s. Their chief assignment was to photograph North Korean and Chinese troop movements. The photos were then used by Allied artillery and aircraft in pinpointing their targets.

The Shooting Star played an active role in the Korean War, both as a fighter and camera plane.

Other Data (Model FP-80A)
Wingspan: 39 ft., 11 in.
Length: 34 ft., 6 in.
Power Plant: One 4,000-lb.-thrust General Electric
 J-33-A-11 turbojet
Loaded Weight: 14,500 lb.
Maximum Speed: 558 mph

LOCKHEED P2V NEPTUNE

The Navy maintains regular vigilance over coastal regions of the United States, using long-range reconnaissance planes equipped with sensitive listening devices. Detecting enemy submarines is the No. 1 job these patrol planes have.

In the early 1940s, the Lockheed Corporation saw the need for an aircraft that would range farther and carry more equipment than any other patrol plane in operation.

Design work on the plane began on December 6, 1941. The next day Japanese forces attacked Pearl Harbor. Other projects suddenly became more urgent. It took until 1945 to develop a prototype of the new aircraft, and it was 1947 before the first models were coming off the assembly line. But once in service, the Neptune—in Roman mythology, Neptune is the god of the sea—became the mainstay of the Navy's patrol operations.

The plane's excellence was obvious even before it began day-to-day operations. During September,

A Lockheed SP-2H, the final production version of the trusty Neptune.

1946, a specially fitted-out version of the aircraft, named the "Truculent Turtle," set a world nonstop record by flying from Perth, Australia, to Columbus, Ohio, a distance of 11,236 miles, without refueling.

Later, on March 7, 1949, a P2V took off from the deck of the aircraft carrier *Coral Sea*. At 74,000 pounds, it established a record weight for a carrier takeoff. Eventually, eleven P2Vs were modified for carrier operations.

Other design changes were made during the 1950s. Turrets containing 20-mm cannons were installed in the plane's nose and atop the fuselage. Another version of the plane was fitted out to carry mines, torpedoes, and depth bombs. Still others were winterized for reconnaissance missions in the Antarctic, where they operated on skis.

The Neptune saw duty in Korea during the Korean War, and special missions were developed for the plane during the Vietnam War. The plane dropped sensors, called spikebuoys, along enemy trails. These were meant to detect vibrations from enemy trucks and other vehicles. The Neptune was able to plant the sensors because of its precision navigational equipment and accurate bombsight. But in dropping the spikebuoys, the Neptune had to fly very low. This put the plane within easy range of enemy antiaircraft fire. Helicopters and F-4 fighters eventually took over the mission.

As a patrol craft, however, the Neptune con-

Some models of the Neptune bristled with 20-mm cannons mounted in nose and dorsal turrets.

tinued to serve the Navy until well into the 1960s. The plane was eventually replaced by the Lockheed P-3 Orion (page 49).

Other Data (Model P2V-3)
Wingspan: 120 ft.
Length: 81 ft., 7 in.
Power Plant: Two 3,250-hp R-3350 Wright
   Cyclones
Loaded Weight: 76,152 lb.
Maximum Speed: 341 mph

Big radome above the fuselage was a striking feature of the Lockheed WV-2 Warning Star.

LOCKHEED WV-1 WARNING STAR

Developed by the Lockheed Corporation for TWA, this stylish plane was one of the most successful commercial airliners ever produced. It was designed to meet TWA's wish for an airliner that was capable of flying coast-to-coast routes of the United States nonstop at speeds of at least 300 miles an hour. On April 17, 1944, the first production model took off from Burbank, California, and flew to National Airport in Washington, D.C., in a few seconds under 6 hours, 58 minutes, a record.

But this was during World War II, and so the first batches of planes produced went to the military to be used as transports. After the war ended in 1945, the Lockheed aircraft that came rolling off the assembly line were purchased by TWA and Pan American Airways. Scores were used on both domestic and international flights. Nicknamed the Constellation, the plane became well known almost everywhere in the world.

Beginning in 1949, the Navy began using the Constellation for early warning missions. Designated the WV-1 and named the Warning Star, the plane's job was to police the coastal areas of the United States, setting up massive electronic barriers, then reporting any aircraft or missiles that pierced the barriers.

The Warning Star was fitted out with huge radomes above and below the fuselage. The radomes carried the plane's radar. The aircraft was also provided with wing-tip fuel tanks. The extra fuel these provided gave the plane greater range.

The Lockheed plane saw service during the war in Vietnam. Its first mission was to maintain a radar patrol over North Vietnam and sound the alarm when Russian-built Ilyushin 11-28 light bombers launched attacks against the South. The Air Force was now operating the Warning Star, and had designated it the EC-121.

The aircraft was also tried as an airborne command and control center for air operations over the North. And it was later assigned to detect enemy truck traffic that filtered south along the Ho Chi Minh Trail.

But the big plane with its huge crew of highly trained specialists had no way of defending itself when attacked by enemy fighters—quick and fast MiGs. The military had to find other planes to replace it.

Other Data (Model WV-2)
Wingspan: 126 ft., 2 in.
Length: 116 ft., 2 in.
Power Plant: Four 3,400-hp Wright R-3350
  Cyclones
Loaded Weight: 143,600 lb.
Maximum Speed: 321 mph at 20,000 ft.

Begun in the 1940s, Warning Star's career continued into the 1960s and included the war in Vietnam.

BOEING RB-47 STRATOJET

Just as fighters were converted for use as reconnaissance planes during World War II and in the years that followed, so, too, were bombers. One was the B-47, a six-engine jet with swept-back wings.

The B-47, and the reconnaissance version, the RB-47, were capable of speeds surpassing 600 miles an hour in level flight. The plane had a relatively short range—3,000 miles—but this could be stretched by refueling the plane in the air.

The RB-47 differed from the B-47 in that its interior spaces had been cleared of bombs and packed solidly with black boxes containing electronic equipment. The plane was manned by a

Powered by six turbojets, the RB-47 had a top speed of 640 miles per hour.

pilot, a copilot, navigator, and three "ravens," a slang term for the specialists who operated the electronic gear.

During the late 1950s, RB-47s were assigned to monitor the northern coastline of the Soviet Union east of Finland. The flights were intended to pinpoint where Soviet fighter planes were based and the locations of radar installations. The Soviet Union monitored Alaska and the Canadian Arctic with planes similar to the RB-47, and with the idea of gathering the same kind of information.

The flights of the RB-47s were different than the U-2 flights (page 56). The RB-47 flights were legal, since they were made over international waters. U-2 overflights of the Soviet Union were not legal.

The fact that the RB-47 flights were legal ones did not prevent a tragedy, however. On July 1, 1960, an American RB-47 on patrol off the northern coast of Norway was shot down by a Russian fighter. Four Americans died as a result of the attack. The two survivors, Capt. John F. R. McKone and Capt. Freeman B. Olmstead, parachuted into the Barents Sea, were taken into custody by the Soviets, and imprisoned in Moscow's dread Lubyanka prison.

The two men were accused of spying. That crime, in the Soviet Union, is punishable by death. The Soviets tried all kinds of trickery and threat of death to get McKone and Olmstead to "confess." But they would not. Several months after their imprisonment, the two men were unexpectedly released.

Other Data (Model B-47E)
Wingspan: 116 ft.
Length: 106 ft., 8 in.
Power Plant: Six 6,000-lb.-thrust General Electric J-47 turbojets
Loaded Weight: 200,000 lb.
Maximum Speed: 640 mph

Massive disc-shaped radome gave the Tracer an unusual appearance.

GRUMMAN E-1 TRACER

Up until the 1950s, the military had two ways of delivering nuclear warheads—by bombs dropped from planes and by missiles launched from sunken shelters—called "silos"—made of steel and concrete.

Then the U.S. Navy developed a third method—a missile-firing submarine. Being nuclear-powered, the submarine could remain submerged for weeks, even months, at a time, concealing itself in the vast undersea world, waiting for the order to launch its weapons. Such submarines were almost impossible to detect, at least by the aircraft available in the years following World War II.

Eventually, the Soviet Union also developed nuclear-powered, missile-firing submarines. Once that happened, the Navy began work on a spy plane that would be capable of detecting these subs.

A completely new type of aircraft was needed. It was to be fitted out with the new and sophisticated radar detection equipment that was becoming available. It was also to be given the capability of firing modern-day weapons, which included air-to-underwater guided missiles.

The plane was planned as a twin-engine, high-wing monoplane. Its radar equipment was to be stored in a dome-shaped compartment in the rear fuselage. Designated the S-2A, the plane made its first flight on December 4, 1952. By the early months of 1954, the aircraft began entering active service. It was nicknamed the Tracker.

The same year, Grumman began to develop a version of the plane that was capable of operating from an aircraft carrier. The result was the E-1 Tracer, a strange-looking aircraft, thanks to a massive disk-shaped radome above the fuselage.

The Tracer also carried sonobuoys, as many as 32 of them. These were special floats that produced sound waves. Once dropped in the water, the signals sent out by the sonobuoys could be used by the E-1 to detect submerged enemy submarines.

The first Tracers were delivered to the fleet in February, 1958. Eventually every aircraft carrier had several of them.

Before the Tracer, the "eyes" of the fleet could not "see" beyond the range of ship radar. But the Tracer, with its ability to operate hundreds of miles ahead of the fleet, could detect enemy submarines beyond the horizon. A new era in anti-submarine warfare had dawned.

Other Data (Model E-1)
Wingspan: 72 ft., 7 in.
Length: 43 ft., 6 in.
Power Plant: Two 1,525-hp Wright Cyclones
Loaded Weight: 26,867 lb.
Maximum Speed: 253 mph

A Grumman E-1 Tracer aboard the aircraft carrier *Intrepid*, now a naval museum in New York.

Camera-equipped Crusaders like this one were capable
of operating at speeds of just over 1,000 miles an hour.

LTV RF-8 CRUSADER

Rugged and dependable, F-8 Crusaders were in action from the beginning in Vietnam. And not merely as supersonic fighters, MiG killers. Camera-equipped Crusaders pierced North Vietnamese airspace on a regular basis to bring back needed information. They proved so valuable that the photoreconnaissance version of the plane outlived its fighter cousin by several years.

The F-8 was designed by the Chance Vought Company in 1952. (Later the company became Ling-Temco-Vought, or LTV.) The plane was a star performer from the very first. On March 25, 1955, when the plane was being tested, it breezed through the speed of sound with the greatest of ease. (The speed of sound can vary from 600 to 790 miles per hour, depending on altitude and temperature.) The aircraft was the first carrier-based plane capable of speeds beyond 1,000 miles per hour.

As a fighter plane, the F-8 carried four forward-firing 20-mm cannons, plus rockets and Sidewinder air-to-air missiles. When the F-8 became a reconnaissance plane, the RF-8, the armament was replaced by cameras. One battery of five cameras shot through bulletproof glass ports in the sides and belly of the plane. Two of these shot straight down, while the other three were placed so as to produce horizon-to-horizon photos.

Flying a reconnaissance mission over heavily protected North Vietnam was always hazardous

This RF-8 Crusader was from the Light Photographic Squadron 63 aboard the aircraft carrier Saratoga.

Low-level reconnaissance photo, taken over North Vietnam, shows heavily damaged railroad bridge.

duty, even though the RF-8 would usually be escorted by an F-8. The camera plane had to fly a straight and level course in order to achieve good photos. This made it a relatively easy target for antiaircraft fire.

Photoreconnaissance Crusaders suffered losses that were three times as great as the Navy's average. Twenty RF-8s were lost during the war, most of them in the period between 1968 and 1971.

Other Data (Model RF-8A)
Wingspan: 35 ft., 8 in.
Length: 54 ft., 3 in.
Power Plant: One 16,000-lb.-thrust Pratt & Whitney J-57 two-shaft turbojet
Loaded Weight: 34,000 lb.
Maximum Speed: 1,013 mph

The last of the Navy's flying boats, the Marlin saw service from 1952 until 1966.

MARTIN P5M MARLIN

It was natural for the Navy to build flying boats, huge, lumbering craft that could take off from and land on the water. Thousands were turned out during World War II to serve as long-range reconnaissance aircraft and bombers.

Flying boats were especially valuable in anti-submarine warfare, and it was for that use that the Martin P5M Marlin, designed and developed in the years following World War II, was intended. Its nose was fashioned into a large radome for search radar. In its enormous hull were several different types of electronic gear for detecting submerged submarines. Cameras were carried in a streamlined pod attached to the outside of the fuselage.

The Marlin also carried all the weapons necessary to attack and destroy enemy submarines—up to 8,000 pounds of bombs, torpedoes, and mines.

The first production model of the Marlin flew on June 22, 1951. The Navy began taking deliveries of the plane the following year. By 1954, 114 Marlins had been built.

An improved version of the aircraft featured a T-shaped tail and better living quarters for the crew. Designated the P5M-2, it was produced during the late 1950s. A total of 145 P5M-2s were eventually turned out.

Martin Marlins saw duty in Vietnam. They patrolled the waters of the Tonkin Gulf until 1965. Some P5M-2s also performed search-and-rescue missions for the U.S. Coast Guard.

The Marlin remained in service until 1966. The Navy had decided to use land-based planes for long-range patrol duty. In addition, helicopters were taking over many of the duties once performed by flying boats. When the last Martin Marlin went into retirement, it marked the end of an era.

Other Data (Model P5M-2)
Wingspan: 118 ft., 2 in.
Length 100 ft., 7 in.
Power Plant: Two 3,450-hp Wright R-3350 Cyclones
Loaded Weight: 85,000 lb.
Maximum Speed: 251 mph at sea level

Big T-shaped tail and bulbous nose radome were design features of the improved version of the Marlin.

39

Crew members aboard aircraft carrier *Forrestal* prepare to launch an E-2 Hawkeye.

GRUMMAN E-2 HAWKEYE

In the Falklands War of 1982, in which Great Britain clashed with Argentina to regain control of the Falkland Islands after they had been invaded by the Argentines, an early victim was a British destroyer, the *Sheffield*. A radar ship, the *Sheffield* was intended to warn the British fleet of approaching enemy aircraft. Flying low at high speeds, Argentine planes bombed the *Sheffield*, and the vessel had to be abandoned.

What the British could have used at the time was a plane such as the Navy's E-2 Hawkeye, an AEW (Airborne Early Warning) aircraft. With its large and very powerful radars, the E-2 can detect airborne targets large and small. In the case of a large target, a fighter or attack plane, the Hawkeye's radar is effective for a distance of up to 230 miles. The Hawkeye also monitors ship movements.

No American aircraft carrier leaves home without some Hawkeyes. They have made extinct radar ships such as the *Sheffield*.

The E-2 is manned by a crew of five—a pilot, copilot, a combat information officer, a radar operator, and an air control officer. As the pilots fly the plane, the other crew members monitor displays and other pieces of information from the radar and thirty other electronic devices. They get a complete picture of as many as 250 targets, plus the tracks or trajectories for each. A mission can last for as long as six hours.

The first E-2 flew on January 20, 1971. The first production models began entering service late in 1973. In the years that followed, production was slow but steady. By 1987, approximately one hundred E-2s were on active duty with the U.S. Navy. Japan, Egypt, Singapore, and Israel have also used the plane.

Wings folded, an E-2 Hawkeye awaits the call to action aboard carrier *Forrestal*.

Pilot aboard carrier *America* checks E-2's prop before takeoff.

Other Data (Model E-2C)
Wingspan: 80 ft., 7 in.
Length: 57 ft., 7 in.
Power Plant: Two 4,910-hp Allison turboprops
Loaded Weight: 51,569 lb.
Maximum Speed: 374 mph

41

GRUMMAN OV-1 MOHAWK

Developed during the late 1950s for battlefield reconnaissance, the OV-1 proved to be a valuable weapon during the Vietnam War. It provided field commanders with the answers to these questions: "Where are the enemy troops?" "How many are there?" "What are they doing?"

While the Mohawk never won any medals for speed or maneuverability, it was well-equipped for the job it was intended to do. It had all-weather navigation and communications equipment. It could land and take off on short runways. It offered its crew members at least some protec-

OV-1 Mohawk is medium size—bigger and more powerful than light aircraft, yet smaller than four-engine planes.

tion against ground fire.

The pilot sat on the left and an observer or equipment operator on the right. The multi-windowed cockpit gave both a commanding view of the battlefield.

The Mohawk could be equipped with a wide variety of reconnaissance gear. Often it carried a special camera that could take horizon-to-horizon photos. Other cameras could concentrate on smaller targets, such as road junctions, hamlets, or clusters of hills. The photographs provided the kind of detail that ground commanders needed.

The Mohawk could also be equipped with SLAR (Side-Looking Airborne Radar), which was housed in a long pod beneath the fuselage. The radar scanned roads used to bring troops and supplies into the battle area. A photographic map was produced from the radar signals while the plane was in flight, pinpointing targets for Air Force attack planes and gunships.

The Mohawk could also monitor battlefield equipment with infrared sensors. Any object—a chair, table, or coffee cup—gives off infrared rays, sometimes called heat rays. Sensing devices pick up infrared rays coming from various objects, and record the images of those objects on film. Like radar, infrared sensors can "see" at night in the dark or through fog. Infrared equipment proved especially valuable in Vietnam, because the North Vietnamese and Viet Cong often depended on darkness to conceal their movements.

The development of SAMs (Surface-to-Air-Missiles) during the early 1960s brought an end to the use of Mohawks as a battlefield weapon. But in the years that followed, the Army continued to use the airplane for intelligence gathering. And as recently as 1983, several OV-1s were supplied to Pakistan to monitor that nation's border with India.

Other Data (Model OV-1D)
Wingspan: 48 ft.
Length: 44 ft., 11 in.
Power Plant: Two 1,160-hp Lycoming 53-701
    turboprops
Loaded Weight: 18,109 lb.
Maximum Speed: 310 mph

Mohawks earned high marks in Vietnam by providing information on enemy troop movements for field commanders.

Long pod beneath the Mohawk's fuselage holds Side-Looking Airborne Radar.

A RA-5C Vigilante from the carrier *Constellation* in flight over the South China Sea.

NORTH AMERICAN RA-5 VIGILANTE

The word "vigilante" was widely used in the American West a century or so ago. It referred to individuals who, taking the law into their own hands, sought to capture and punish those they believed to be guilty of criminal behavior.

In a sense, the first A-5s fitted that definition. They were strictly attack aircraft, meant to "punish" the enemy. They played no role as intelligence gatherers.

The first production model A-5s were supplied to the aircraft carrier *Enterprise* in 1962. They were big planes, the heaviest, in fact, ever to see service aboard American carriers, with the exception of the Douglas A-3 Skywarrior. The Vigilantes were also powerful and fast, capable of traveling at more than twice the speed of sound.

The Vigilante's bomb bay was intended for nuclear weapons to which the plane's extra fuel tanks were attached. The Vigilante burned the fuel on its way to the target, then dropped the tanks along with the bombs. The empty tanks acted to keep each of the bombs on target as they headed earthward.

The Vigilante, however, never saw action as an attack plane. There were problems in getting the plane's bomb bay system to work properly. Before the problems could be solved, the Navy's role in strategic bombing was erased.

It was then decided to make the Vigilante a reconnaissance plane. The letter R was added to its designation. The first RA-5s were assigned to the carrier *Ranger* in 1964.

During the war in Vietnam, Vigilantes took off from carriers in the Gulf of Tonkin to gather intelligence on the heavily defended areas of North Vietnam. Some flew at high altitudes; others skimmed the surface of the earth. The RA-5 was especially effective in photographing missile sites. Each photo carried a notation as to the exact location of the site, expressed in longitude and latitude. That made it easy for attack planes to pinpoint their targets.

The Vigilante could also be equipped with SLAR (Side-Looking Airborne Radar) and infrared sensing equipment. And some Vigilantes were fitted with extra fuel packs, reels, and hoses, which enabled them to serve other aircraft as "buddy" tankers.

Launching an RA-5C Vigilante from No. 1 catapult of the carrier *Saratoga*.

Other Data (Model RA-5C)
Wingspan: 53 ft.
Length: 76 ft., 6 in.
Power Plant: Two 10,800-lb.-thrust General Electric J79-GE-8 turbojets
Loaded Weight: 79,588 lb.
Maximum Speed: Mach 2.1; 1,385 mph at 40,000 ft.

LOCKHEED S-3 VIKING

Beginning in 1967, the Navy saw the need for a carrier-based search-and-strike aircraft to replace the E-1 Tracer and S-2 Tracker in antisubmarine warfare. Several aircraft manufacturers were asked to submit designs for the new plane. Lockheed's design won the competition.

The Lockheed plans called for a compact, high-wing monoplane. It was to be powered by a pair of turbofan engines that were to be housed in underwing pods.

An S-3 Viking antisubmarine aircraft lifts from the deck of the carrier *Forrestal*.

The Viking carried a great variety of electronic equipment, including several different types of sensors and navigation radars. In addition, the plane had electronic metal detectors and 60 sonobuoys, plus the equipment to keep track of them once they were dropped. There were also computers aboard.

Once the Viking had spotted an enemy submarine, it had the weapons to destroy it. Bombs, depth charges, torpedoes, and ASMs (Anti-Submarine Missiles) were carried within the plane in a weapons bay. A pair of underwing pylons held rockets and missiles.

A four-man crew was required. Besides the pilot, it included a copilot, a sensor operator, and a tactical control coordinator.

A test model of the S-3 flew in November, 1971. Production models were being assigned to aircraft carriers by 1974. The first went to the *Forrestal*. The Viking continued to serve the fleet well into the 1980s.

Other Data (Model S-3A)
Wingspan: 68 ft., 8 in.
Length: 58 ft., 4 in.
Power Plant: Two 9,275-lb.-thrust General
    Electric TF34-GE-2 turbofans
Loaded Weight: 52,539 lb.
Maximum Speed: 514 mph

Though neither sleek nor graceful, the Viking has a maximum speed of 514 miles per hour. It can operate at altitudes of up to 35,000 feet.

S-3's wing tips fold back for flight deck parking.

A P-3 Orion in flight near Jacksonville, Florida.

LOCKHEED P-3 ORION

During the 1970s and 1980s, Lockheed's P-3 Orion ranked as the Navy's No. 1 land-based aircraft in terms of electronic reconnaissance.

Its spacious fuselage was filled with special detection radars, other electronic sensing systems, and sophisticated data processing equipment. Its bomb bay carried a wide variety of weapons, including torpedoes, mines, and nuclear depth bombs. Mines and rockets were also carried under its wings. A crew of ten was required to operate the plane and its equipment.

The P-3 had its beginnings in 1957 when the Navy began seeking a replacement plane for the P2V Neptune. Several manufacturers were asked to submit designs for the new plane.

At the time, Lockheed was supplying some of the nation's airlines with a four-engine turboprop aircraft named the Electra. The company took an Electra and made it over in keeping with what the Navy wanted in the way of a new patrol plane. The Electra's fuselage was shortened by about 7 feet and a big weapons bay was added. The new airplane was successfully tested in 1959.

The plane was given the name Orion in 1960. In Greek mythology, Orion is a hunter. Eventually slain, Orion was placed in the sky as a constellation. The name was chosen for the P-3 to emphasize the plane's role in hunting enemy submarines.

One of the sensor stations aboard a P-3 Orion.

No other aircraft is better equipped for that mission.

The first P-3s, designated P-3As, were delivered to their naval units in 1962. On patrol, the aircraft cruised at 230-240 miles per hour at an altitude of

A P-3 Orion flies in formation with a Douglas EA-3 Skywarrior.

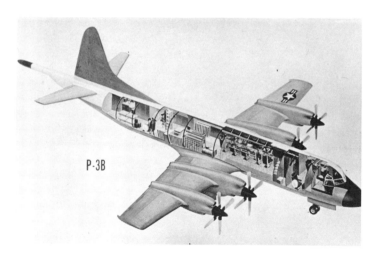

P-3B

A cutaway view of the P-3 Orion. It takes a ten-man crew to operate the plane and its equipment.

about 1,500 feet. The plane's maximum speed was 473 miles an hour. Each of the plane's patrol missions lasted about three hours.

The P-3A was followed by the P-3B and P-3C. By the mid-1970s, the Navy had received about 180 Orions and was ordering about twelve additional planes each year.

Lockheed continued to upgrade the plane. One improvement concerned the plane's radar, which could scan only forward. In 1985, Lockheed introduced a P-3 with a big saucer-shaped rotodome that was fixed to the top of the plane's fuselage. (A rotodome is a rotating radome.) The addition of the rotodome enabled the Orion's radar to scan in a full circle; it could, in other words, cover all points of the compass.

New data and communications equipment were also developed for the Orion. This included equipment that made possible communications with orbiting satellites.

During the late 1980s, P-3 Orions took on a new role. The Navy and the U.S. Customs Service began using the aircraft (and also the E-2C Hawkeye) over American coastal waters in an effort to spot aircraft and ships and boats involved in illegal drug smuggling.

The drug problem was very serious. In April, 1986, President Ronald Reagan instructed the military to look upon drugs as a threat to national security. Congress considered the Department of Defense Narcotics Assistance Act. The bill would provide $440 million for aircraft to be used in fighting drug traffic. The P-3 Orion will be one of the planes in the forefront of the struggle.

A P-3 takes off from a runway at the U.S. Naval Station, Roosevelt Roads, Puerto Rico.

Other Data (Model P-3C)
Wingspan: 99 ft., 8 in.
Length: 116 ft., 10 in.
Power Plant: Four 4,910-hp Allison T56-A-14
    turboprops
Loaded Weight: 135,000 lb.
Maximum Speed: 473 mph

This P-3, based at the Jacksonville, Florida, Naval Air Station, is used as a weather reconnaissance plane.

E-3's disc-shaped radome is 30 feet in diameter.

BOEING E-3 SENTRY

In the early 1900s, President Theodore Roosevelt ordered sixteen American battleships to make an around-the-world cruise. Known as the "Great White Fleet" (because all Navy ships of the day were painted white), the vessels sailed from Hampton Roads, Virginia, in December, 1907.

The mission of the Great White Fleet was to boost the prestige of the United States. The ships

52

were also meant to help ease tensions in the Far East, where the United States and Japan were in conflict over trade policies.

Everywhere the ships went the officers and crew members were warmly greeted. The show of naval strength helped calm troubled waters in the Far East.

In recent years, when American presidents have been faced with hostilities in the Middle East, they have acted as President Theodore Roosevelt did. But instead of sending warships to the trouble spots, they often send airplanes—E-3 Sentry AWACS planes. (AWACS stands for Airborne Warning and Control System.)

The E-3 Sentry was derived from the Boeing 707, an airliner that was well known in commercial service. But unlike the 707, the E-3 has a disc-shaped radome, 30 feet in diameter, mounted on top of its fuselage on a pair of struts that are 14 feet in height.

Each E-3 is crammed with four tons of radar equipment, the latest in communications technology, and a high-speed computer. This equipment enables the E-3 to scan vast expanses of land and sea and give defending forces warning of aircraft that are up to 200 miles away.

The E-3 can track as many as 400 aircraft at a time. Thanks to its giant IFF (Identification Friend or Foe) system, the Sentry is able to identify each plane as friendly or otherwise. In the case of enemy aircraft, it tells pilots where to meet each attacker and the route to take to get there.

Jimmy Carter was the first American president to use AWACS aircraft to help cool international tensions. In March, 1979, Carter sent two E-3s to Saudi Arabia. War had broken out between North Yemen, a nation friendly to Saudi Arabia, and South Yemen. The E-3s were used to police the skies over North Yemen.

Carter used AWACS aircraft a number of other

Computer consoles aboard an E-3 Sentry.

An E-3 AWACS aircraft in the skies over the western Pacific island of Okinawa.

times during his administration. He sent them as a warning to North Korea when political strife threatened our ally, South Korea. He ordered E-3s to West Germany at the time the Soviet Union seemed on the brink of invading Poland.

President Reagan sent E-3s to Egypt in 1981 after the assassination of President Anwar Sadat. Egyptian leaders feared the country might be attacked by Libya, Egypt's neighbor to the West. The E-3s were handed the job of monitoring air-

space near Libya. There was no attack.

Four AWACS planes have seen duty with the Saudi Arabian Air Force. Their effectiveness was demonstrated on June 5, 1984, over the Persian Gulf. An AWACS command post spotted Iranian jets as they took off, and warned the Saudi control center. F-15 Eagle fighter planes were sent up to intercept the Iranian aircraft. The AWACS plane guided the Saudi pilots to their targets. Once the battle began, the AWACS crew stood guard against attacks by other Iranian planes. Two Iranian F-4 jets were destroyed.

The Sentry can fly at high speeds for as long as eleven hours. With in-flight refueling from tankers, the plane can stay aloft for days at a time.

The E-3 Sentry made its first flight on February 5, 1972. Approximately thirty-five E-3s were in service by the mid-1980s. Eighteen more had been ordered by NATO, the North Atlantic Treaty Organization. The Sentry has also seen duty in Europe, Iceland, and Okinawa, besides the Middle East.

Military experts predict that AWACS aircraft will continue to be effective in command and communications for another decade or more.

Planes such as the E-3 Sentry carry no standard weapons. Yet what they do carry enables these aircraft to change the course of a battle or a war. And they can play a bigger role in keeping peace than the most heavily armed ships or planes.

Other Data (Model E-3A)
Wingspan: 145 ft., 9 in.
Length: 152 ft., 11 in.
Power Plant: Four 21,000-lb.-thrust Pratt &
    Whitney turbofans
Loaded Weight: 325,000 lb.
Maximum Speed: 627 mph (estimate)

Experts expect the E-3 to continue to play an important role in military surveillance well into the 1990s.

With its big wing and long thin body, the U-2 looks like a sailplane.

LOCKHEED U-2, TR-1

During the 1950s, the United States and the Soviet Union were locked in a "cold war." There was great rivalry and tension between the two nations, although it stopped short of an armed conflict.

United States intelligence experts sought to learn all they could about Soviet military activities. Secret aircraft loaded with cameras and sensing devices were sent over the Soviet Union to gather information.

But the Soviet Union covers a sizeable chunk of the globe, and the planes available did not have the range to penetrate safely to the Soviet interior. When they tried, the planes were peppered with fire from Soviet surface-to-air missiles.

The Central Intelligence Agency (CIA), the federal agency that oversees U.S. intelligence activities, sought to overcome this problem in 1953 by asking the Lockheed Corporation to develop an aircraft that could cover great distances non-stop. It would also have to have the ability to fly higher than Soviet missiles could reach. The result was the U-2. The plane was first flown on August 1, 1955.

CIA officials were very pleased with the U-2. It could cruise at an altitude between 68,000 and 72,000 feet. Soviet missiles were not effective above 60,000 feet. That meant the U-2 would have a zone of from 8,000 to 12,000 feet in which it could safely operate.

The first overflight of the Soviet Union took place during the summer of 1956. A CIA pilot was at the controls. Other flights followed. A typical flight would take off from Peshawar, Pakistan, fly for nine hours across the forbidden territory of the Soviet Union, and land in Bodø, Norway.

President Dwight D. Eisenhower was uneasy about the flights. For one nation to violate the airspace of another during peacetime is serious business. The President feared that if the Soviets discovered what was going on it might even trigger a nuclear war.

Eisenhower thought of what might happen if the situation happened to be reversed, if it was discovered that the Soviet Union was sending military aircraft from Canada to Mexico over the heartland of the United States. The American peo-ple would be shocked. Congress might ask for a declaration of war.

Despite his worries, Eisenhower continued to approve the flights. The Soviet air defense system tracked the flights but they were helpless to do anything about them.

In 1960, the situation began to change. The Soviets had developed new, more powerful rockets.

Meanwhile, the cold war was beginning to thaw a bit. Russian Premier Nikita Khrushchev had visited the United States and met with Eisenhower at Camp David. The two men had become friendly. In May, 1960, Eisenhower was scheduled to meet

A U-2 takes off on a pre-dawn training mission from Beale Air Force Base, California.

Khrushchev in Paris along with the leaders of Great Britain and France. A chance to ease tensions loomed. The following month, Eisenhower was set to go to the Soviet Union to visit Khrushchev. A big welcome was being planned.

Even as the summit meeting between Eisenhower and Khrushchev was drawing near, the U-2 flights continued. Then disaster struck. On May 1, 1960, over the city of Sverdlovsk, Soviet missiles brought down a U-2. The pilot, Francis Gary Powers, parachuted and survived.

Khrushchev was boiling mad. At the summit meeting in Paris two weeks later, he was still fuming. He demanded an apology for the spy plane flights. Eisenhower refused. The summit conference blew up and with it any hopes for im-

Though not a particularly fast plane, the U-2 could climb high, and was able to operate at altitudes of up to 72,000 feet.

The TR-1 was similar to the U-2, but featured wing pods used for the storage of extra fuel.

proving relations with the Soviets. Eisenhower never made his visit to Russia. He returned to the United States a much saddened man.

Francis Gary Powers, the U-2 pilot, was tried and convicted of spying. He was later exchanged for a Soviet spy held in the United States.

The U-2 was headlines again in 1962. President John F. Kennedy, concerned that the Soviet Union might be sending military supplies to Cuba, ordered U-2s to fly over the island once a week. Sites for missile-launchers and the missiles themselves were photographed.

During the war in Vietnam, U-2s made an important contribution. They photographed enemy missile defenses and Soviet fighter planes and bombers.

In 1968, a new version of the U-2 was introduced. Designated the U-2R, it offered wing pods containing extra fuel. A still later version of the plane, with side-scanning radar, was designated the TR-1.

During the mid-1980s, approximately twenty TR-1s were based in Alconbury, England, and West Germany. Where they went and what they did was top secret. But it was not believed that any of the planes ever overflew the Soviet Union.

Other Data (Model U-2A)
Wingspan: 80 ft.
Length: 49 ft., 7 in.
Power Plant: One Pratt & Whitney 11,200-lb.-
    thrust J-57-13A turbojet
Loaded Weight: 11,700 lb.
Maximum Speed: 494 mph

SR-71 was designed, built, and test-flown in total secrecy.

LOCKHEED SR-71 BLACKBIRD

During the summer of 1974, the U.S. Air Force decided to try to break the world's record for a flight from New York to London. At the time, the record was 4 hours and 40 minutes. It had been set by a Royal Navy F-4 Phantom in 1969.

The plane the Air Force chose for the attempt was the SR-71 Blackbird, believed to be the fastest, highest-flying aircraft ever built. At two minutes after midnight on September 1 of that year, an SR (for Strategic Reconnaissance)-71 lifted off the long runway at Beale Air Force Base not far from Marysville in northern California, climbed high into the night sky and headed east. Major James V. Sullivan was at the controls. Major Noel F. Widdifield, serving as reconnaissance safety officer, or RSO, was seated in the cockpit behind Sullivan.

At 26,000 feet over the Nevada desert, the plane took on a full load of fuel from a KC-135 tanker plane. Sullivan then took the Blackbird higher and accelerated to Mach 3 for the flight across the United States. A second refueling was required, and this took place over the Atlantic Ocean near the coast of North Carolina. Then Sullivan advanced the throttle once more, nosed the big plane upward and pushed its speed to Mach 3 again. The plane flashed by its checkpoint just east of New York City and sped for London.

Beale Air Force Base near Marysville, California, is home base for the SR-71.

In about the time it takes a passenger car to travel from New York to Philadelphia, the sound of the Blackbird's engines could be heard over the English coast. Exactly 1 hour, 55 minutes, and 42 seconds after passing through the New York timing gate, the SR-71 crossed a similar checkpoint near Southhampton, England. It had traveled at an average speed of 1,806.964 miles an hour. Sullivan had not merely broken the record, he had sliced it in half.

In the years that followed, the Blackbird claimed many other records. These included:

• Speed over a recognized course, London to Los Angeles (September 13, 1974)—1,435.587 miles per hour.

• Speed over a closed course (July 28, 1976)—2,193.167 miles per hour.

• Altitude on a horizontal flight (July 28, 1976)—85,068.997 feet. 16 mile

Aside from the speed and altitude records the

SR-71 gets its nickname—Blackbird—from its very dark blue-black paint scheme.

Blackbird has set, not much is known about the aircraft. It was a project that was shrouded in secrecy from the beginning. The plane was meant to be the successor to the U-2, but be capable of flying higher and at a faster speed. Almost unbelievably, the Lockheed Corporation managed to design, build, and flight-test early models of the plane, and not let anyone know about it.

There were enormous problems to be overcome in designing the SR-71. Many of these resulted from the extremely high temperatures generated by flying at three times the speed of sound (Mach 3) for long periods of time. Skin temperatures of the plane ranged from 450° to 1200° F. As a result, the plane had to be built almost entirely of tough tintanium alloys.

Electrical connectors had to be gold-plated to protect them from heat damage. New fuels, lubricants, and insulating materials had to be developed.

The high skin temperatures the plane generated were the reason it was painted black. Black paint helped to radiate the heat away from the plane's surface.

President Lyndon Johnson revealed the existence of the SR-71 in February, 1964. The plane, designated the YF-12A at the time, had its first public showing at Edwards Air Force Base in California later that year.

While the Air Force would not reveal any details about the Blackbird, bits and pieces of information leaked out concerning its tremendous speed and range. It was learned, for example, that the SR-71 could survey a strip of ground thirty miles wide, from Los Angeles to Washington, D.C.— *and do it in an hour.*

During the late 1960s and throughout the 1970s, all of the world's trouble spots were monitored by the SR-71. Vietnam, the Middle East, and Cuba were photographed on a regular basis by SR-71s flying from England, Okinawa, and Thailand.

SR-71s were said to have mapped the entire Chinese mainland, a project that required hundreds of overflights. When President Richard Nixon sought to visit China in 1972 on a peace-

Blackbird's twin afterburners glow in the night sky.

keeping mission, he agreed to stop the SR-71 flights.

The Air Force has never announced how many SR-71s it has in operation. The number is believed to be about twenty, however. They operate in utmost secrecy. They continue to rank as the fastest, highest-flying aircraft in the world.

Other Data (Model SR-71C)
Wingspan: 55 ft., 7 in.
Length: 107 ft., 51 in.
Power Plant: Two 32,500-lb.-thrust Pratt &
    Whitney J-58 afterburning turbojets
Loaded Weight: 170,000 lb.
Maximum Speed: Mach 3 plus

SPYCRAFT IN SPACE

Modern spy planes such as the SR-71 Blackbird and U-2 do not have a bright future. They're slowly being replaced by the nation's growing fleet of spy satellites.

"Satellites go where aircraft can't," says one intelligence expert. "That includes most of the world. And because satellite reconnaissance is so good, the use of aircraft is declining."

The new era in aerial spying began during the late 1950s when the CIA and Air Force began developing a satellite that could take over for the U-2. That satellite, named Discoverer, became a reality in 1960. After being sent into orbit above the earth, the spacecraft's cameras took pictures of the Soviet Union. The capsule containing the exposed film was then ejected by the satellite. As the film parachuted to earth, it was plucked from the air by a plane trailing a special trapezelike rigging.

Since that beginning, the spy satellite program has exploded in size. Just about every square inch of land, sea, air, and space is under surveillance today.

Active spy satellites include:

• KH-11—The largest and most sophisticated of the spy satellites, it travels at an altitude of between 170 and 300 miles. It is used for full-time surveillance.

• KH-12—An improved version of KH-11, this satellite can come down as low as 70 miles for a close look. An object on the ground as small as a ballpoint pen can be distinguished in its photos.

• Big Bird—A massive satellite used for photography and electronic eavesdropping.

• White Cloud—A satellite that watches the oceans with radar, radio, and infrared sensors, tracking surface ships and submarines.

• Rhyolite—Eavesdrops on communications and electronic signals, including transmissions from Russian launches.

While the important spying is done by satellites, high-flying reconnaissance planes still have a role to play. Planes such as the SR-71 and U-2 are ordered into the air when more information on a specific target is needed. And sometimes they're called upon when cloud cover interferes with the satellite operation. Don't count out the spy plane yet.